THE GREAT MARTYRS OF KARBALA

Colouring and Activity Book

Fasiha Zehara

Muharram is the first month of the Islamic calendar. During this month, Imam Hussain (AS) and his companions were martyred by the wicked ruler Yazid. The martyrs of Karbala were the loyal companions, friends and family members of Imam Hussain (AS). They give us inspiration and teach us many important life lessons, so let's learn about the roles they played in the Battle of Karbala.

HAZRAT HURR IBN AL-RIYAHI was the commander of the Yazidi army who was sent to fight with Imam Hussain (AS). On the night of Ashura, he felt sorry for his actions and asked forgiveness from Imam Hussain (AS). The Imam forgave him. On the day of Ashura, Hazrat Hurr was martyred while fighting against the soldiers of Yazid.

Lesson: The lesson we learn from Hazrat Hurr's story is that even if we commit great sins but repent sincerely, Allah (SWT) would still forgive us. It is never too late to ask forgiveness, and we must not lose hope in the mercy of Allah.

Hazrat Hurr (AS)

HAZRAT HABIB IBN MAZAHIR was a childhood friend of Imam Hussain (AS). During the battle at Karbala, when Imam Hussain (AS) was left alone, he wrote a letter to Habib requesting his help. When Habib received the letter from the imam, he rushed to Karbala and fought bravely against the army of Yazid. He was martyred at the age of 75.

Lesson: The story of Hazrat Habib ibn Mazahir teaches us the value of true friendship and loyalty. We must ask ourselves if we are also helping your friends during their difficult times or if we are leaving them alone?

Hazrat Habib (AS)

HAZRAT AUN & HAZRAT MOHAMMED were the brave and obedient sons of Bibi Zainab (S.A). On the night before Ashura, their mother told them that they were too young to fight but if anything happens to Imam Hussain (AS) in their presence, then she will be ashamed.

The young boys couldn't let their mother down. On the day of Ashura, they fought so bravely at such a tender age and at last, attained martyrdom, making their mother proud.

Lesson: A beautiful lesson that we learn from the story of Aun & Mohammad (AS) is that we must try our best to be a source of pride for our parents and must never let them down in any situation. Do we always respect and obey your parents, especially our mother?

HAZRAT AUN (AS) & HAZRAT MOHAMMED (AS)

HAZRAT QASSIM was the youngest son of Imam Hassan (AS) and was only thirteen years old. He wanted to go to the battlefield to help Imam Hussain (AS) but Imam did not allow this. Feeling sad, he asked his mother for help, so she gave him his father's letter in which it was written:

'O' my son, Qasim, when you see your uncle, Hussain (AS) in Karbala,

lonely and without any helper, don't hesitate in helping him."

When he showed this letter to Imam Hussain (AS), Imam gave him permission to fight. Hazrat Qasim fought so bravely that even Yazid's troops were surprised. The cowardly soldiers attacked him on all sides, and he was martyred.

Lesson: Hazrat Qasim (AS) teaches us that we must respect and obey our elders in all conditions and we must always seek their permission before doing anything.

Hazrat Qasim (AS)

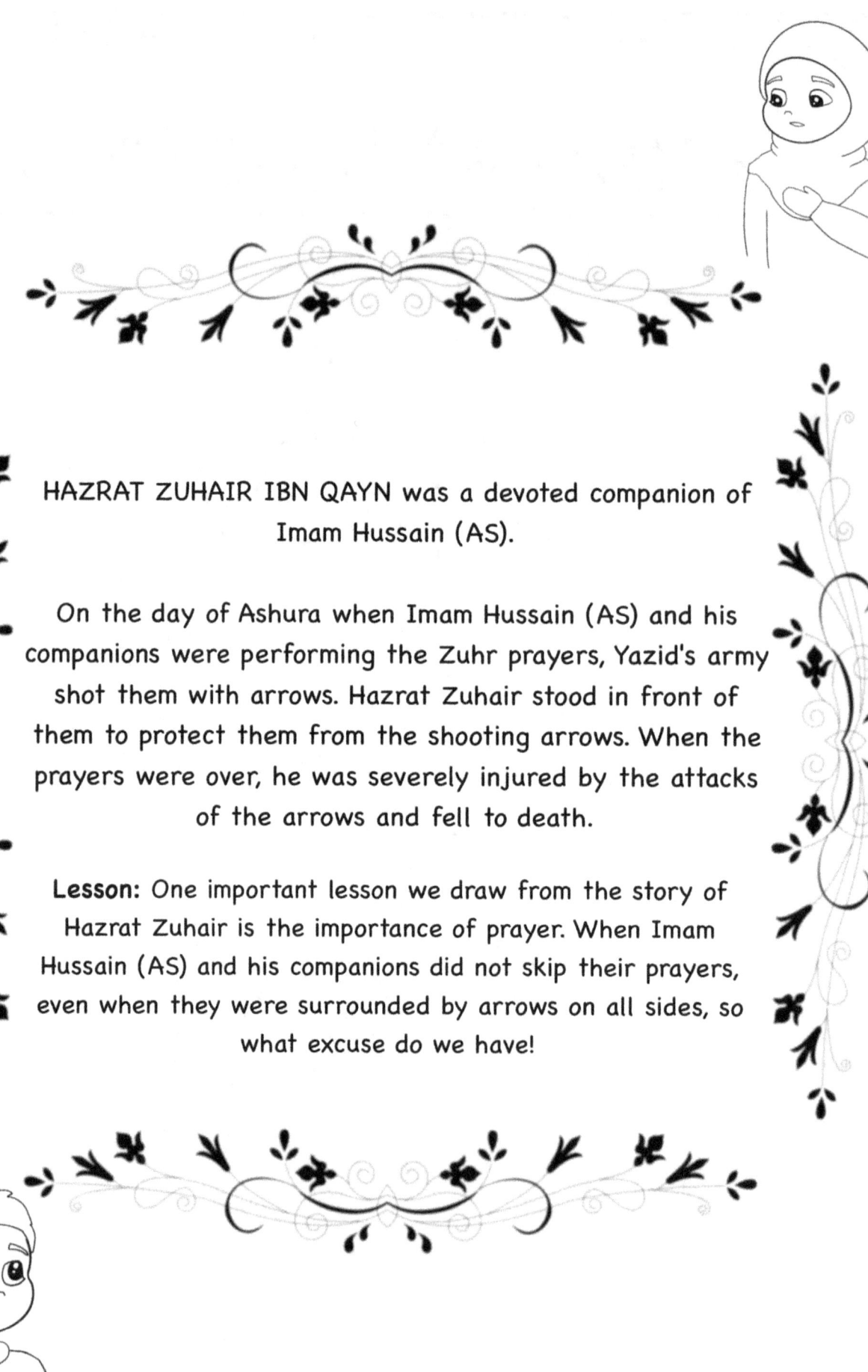

HAZRAT ZUHAIR IBN QAYN was a devoted companion of Imam Hussain (AS).

On the day of Ashura when Imam Hussain (AS) and his companions were performing the Zuhr prayers, Yazid's army shot them with arrows. Hazrat Zuhair stood in front of them to protect them from the shooting arrows. When the prayers were over, he was severely injured by the attacks of the arrows and fell to death.

Lesson: One important lesson we draw from the story of Hazrat Zuhair is the importance of prayer. When Imam Hussain (AS) and his companions did not skip their prayers, even when they were surrounded by arrows on all sides, so what excuse do we have!

Hazrat Zuhair (AS)

HAZRAT ALI AKBAR was the son of Imam Husayn (AS), who was very similar to Prophet Muhammad (S) in appearance. He had a beautiful voice, and it was he who always recited Adhan.

On the morning of the Ashura, Ali Akbar (AS) recited the Adhan for a final time and asked his father for permission to go to the battlefield. Imam Hussain (AS), with much grief, allowed him. He fought very bravely and was martyred by Shimr, the evil soldier of Yazid's army

Lesson: Here again, we learn how important it is to ask our parents for permission. Ali Akbar (AS), even when he wanted to fight for a good cause, first took his father's permission and then only went to battle.

Hazrat Ali Akbar (AS)

HAZRAT ABBAS was the brother of Imam Hussain (AS) and also the Flag-bearer of his army. He was known for his deep foresight, strong faith, loyalty and bravery.

On the day of Ashura, Imam Hussain (AS) sent him to fetch water for the children of Karbala. When he came to the river, he was very thirsty himself but did not drink water, knowing that Imam Hussain (AS) and the children were very thirsty.

The Yazeedi army attacked him from all sides and he lost his both arms. He then fell from his horse and was martyred in Imam Hussain's (AS) lap.

Lesson: An important lesson we learn here is that we must always put others before ourselves. Hazrat Abbas (AS) was very thirsty but he didn't even drink a drop of water, knowing that Imam Hussain (AS) and the children were also thirsty. Such was his loyalty! He was very obedient to Imam of his time and we should learn to become like him to the Imam our time.

Hazrat Abbas (AS)

HAZRAT ALI ASGHAR was the six-month-old son of Imam Hussain (AS) and the youngest martyr in Karbala. He was very thirsty as his mother couldn't give him milk. Imam Hussain (AS) took him to the battlefield to request water, but instead, Hurmula fired an arrow at the baby's neck, and he was martyred in his father's arms.

Lesson: Here, we learn that we must never give up in the face of calamities. The martyrdom of Ali Asghar (AS) was one of the most difficult moments in Imam Hussain's (AS) life, still he didn't lose his courage and sacrificed his beloved baby in the way of Allah.

Hazrat Ali Asghar (AS)

Imam Hussain (AS) was the son of Imam Ali (AS) and grandson of the Prophet Mohammed (S). He was the greatest martyr of Karbala who sacrificed himself and his family for the sake of Islam.

He made the ultimate sacrifice and stood against the wicked ruler Yazid and his army of over 30,000 after being thirsty for three days.

Lesson: Karbala teaches us the universal lesson that we must bravely stand against falsehood, even if we have to make sacrifices.

Karbala teaches us to never support injustice and oppression, regardless of the power of the oppressor.

Karbala teaches us to be patient in the face of calamities, as Imam Hussain (AS) and his companions.

The epic legacy of Karbala lives on until today and inspires millions of people around the world.

Imam Hussain (AS)

Activities

Great Warriors of Karbala

```
D H E K G E D F U Q M Q A Q C D D M
M O H A M M E D X W N A T W Z E H N
I A L I A S G H A R T L V H F B A K
S S C C Z K X A S Y H I A N U D B F
V Z V C F M C Q D M L A P U N B I D
F A I T Z F O H O W Q K Z C N M B A
X B E Y F N Z V M C T B H A M F O T
E B R Y S Z U H A I R A D U X D M M
M A M X H U S S A I N R T S R S G U
D S V C N W T Z Z H Z O V C Q R A F
U F W S Y L E T D E V O C T A F B O
Z K S U C L H O Q A S I M M U M G E
```

Find the following words in the puzzle.
Words are hidden → ↓ and ↘ .

ABBAS	HABIB	QASIM
ALIAKBAR	HURR	ZUHAIR
ALIASGHAR	HUSSAIN	
AUN	MOHAMMED	

Did you know that "Labbaik Ya Hussain" means we are at your service O Hussain"?

We are answering the call of Imam Hussain (AS) when he asked "Is there anyone left to help me?" on the day of Ashura in Karbala.

Part of this means to follow the path of Imam Hussain (AS), to go against oppression, injustice, falsehood and to follow the right path. We should avoid sins and do only good deeds by following the Quran and our holy Ahlulbayt (AS).

Let's take an oath to follow the path of Imam Hussain (AS) and try to be like his companions for the Imam of our time.

Trace your palm and write 'Labbaik Ya Hussain'

**Labbaik
Ya Hussain**

CONNECT THE DOTS

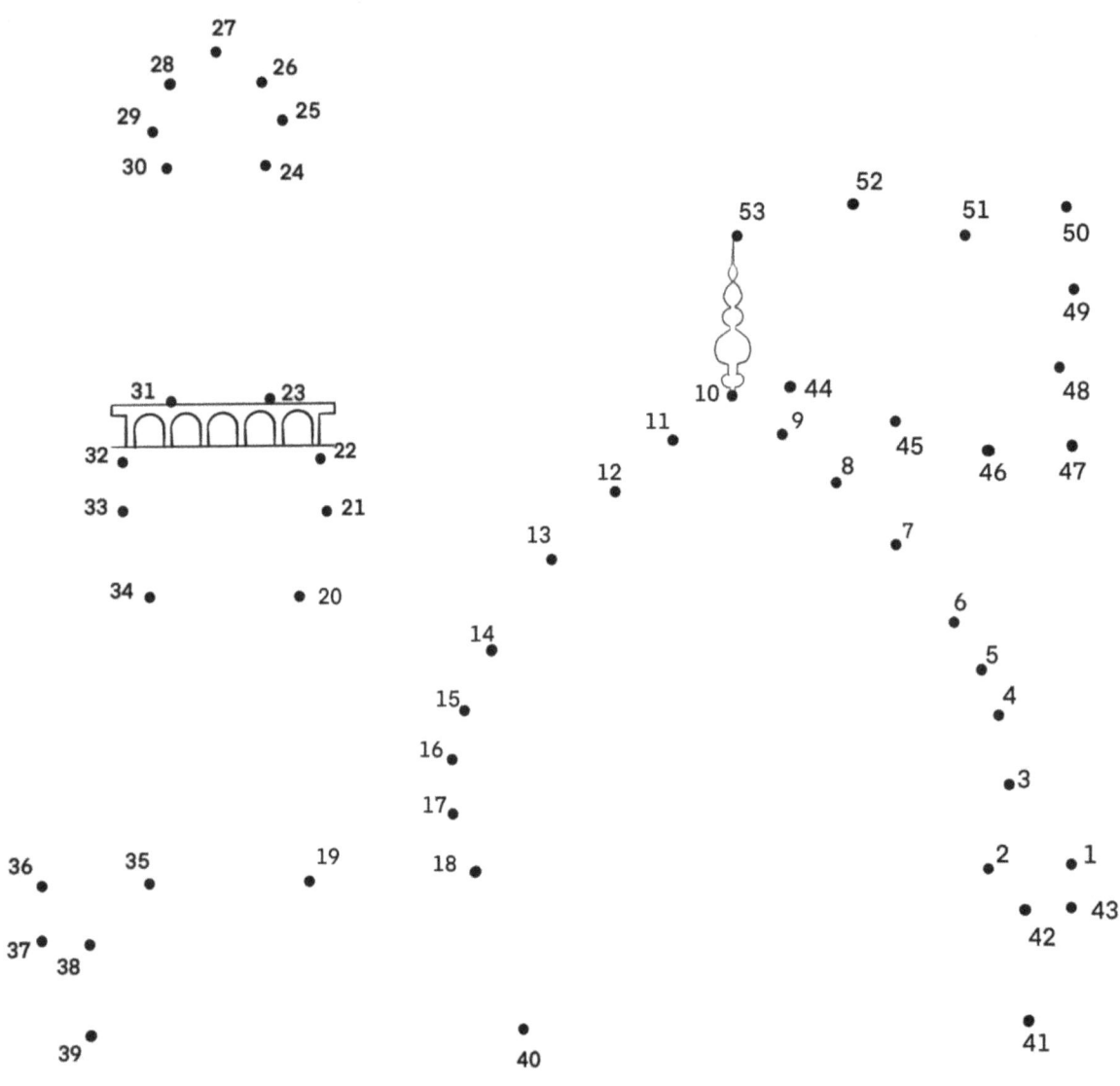

The Holy Shrine of Imam Hussain (AS) in Karbala

Find Your Path To Karbala

Karbala

www.ingramcontent.com/pod-product-compliance
Lightning Source LLC
Chambersburg PA
CBHW080852120626
46546CB00009B/2804